National Landmarks

The Vietnam Veterans Memorial

by Muriel L. Dubois

Consultant:
Tricia Edwards
Program Director
Vietnam Veterans Memorial Fund

Bridgestone Books
an imprint of Capstone Press
Mankato, Minnesota

Bridgestone Books are published by Capstone Press
151 Good Counsel Drive, P.O. Box 669, Mankato, Minnesota 56002
http://www.capstone-press.com

Library of Congress Cataloging-in-Publication Data
Dubois, Muriel L.
  The Vietnam Veterans Memorial/by Muriel L. Dubois.
  p. cm. —(National landmarks)
  Includes bibliographical references and index.
  Summary: Discusses the history of the Vietnam Veterans Memorial, its designer,
  construction of the memorial, its location, and its importance to the people of the
  United States.
  ISBN 0-7368-1116-8
  1. Vietnam Veterans Memorial (Washington, D.C.)—Juvenile literature. [1. Vietnam
  Veterans Memorial (Washington, D.C.) 2. National monuments.] I. Title. II. Series.
DS559.83 W18 D83 2002
959.704′36—dc21   2001003304

Editorial Credits
Erika Mikkelson, editor; Karen Risch, product planning editor; Linda Clavel, cover designer
  and interior layout designer; Erin Scott, illustrator, SARIN Creative; Alta Schaffer,
  photo researcher

Photo Credits
Digital Stock, cover, 1, 6
Guido Alberto Rossi/Archive Photos, 8
Hulton Getty/Getty Images, 16
Janet Sommer/Archive Photos, 18
Jeff Greenberg/Visuals Unlimited, 20
Michael Evans/The Image Finders, 14
Photo by Carol Diehl, 4
Photo courtesy of the Vietnam Veterans Memorial Fund, 10
Reuters/Brian Synder/Archive Photos, 12

1 2 3 4 5 6 07 06 05 04 03 02

Table of Contents

Fast Facts

Three monuments make up the Vietnam Veterans Memorial.

The Wall

The Wall has two parts and is shaped like a "V." Each part has 74 panels. Two panels are blank and 72 panels have the names of Vietnam War veterans on them. In 2001, 58,226 names were on The Wall. Veterans may die from an injury they recieved while serving in the Vietnam War. The veterans' names then are added to The Wall.

★ **Construction Material:** The Wall is made of black granite.

★ **Length:** It is 493 feet, 4 inches (150.4 meters) long.

★ **Height:** It is 10 feet, 1.5 inches (3.09 meters) high at its tallest point.

★ **Cost:** It cost $4,284,000 to build.

The Three Servicemen statue

★ **Construction Material:** The statue is made of bronze.

★ **Height:** The statue is 7 feet (2.13 meters) tall.

★ **Cost:** The statue cost about $4 million.

The Vietnam Women's Memorial

★ **Construction Material:** This statue is made of bronze.

★ **Height:** It is 8 feet (2.4 meters) high.

★ **Cost:** It cost $4 million.

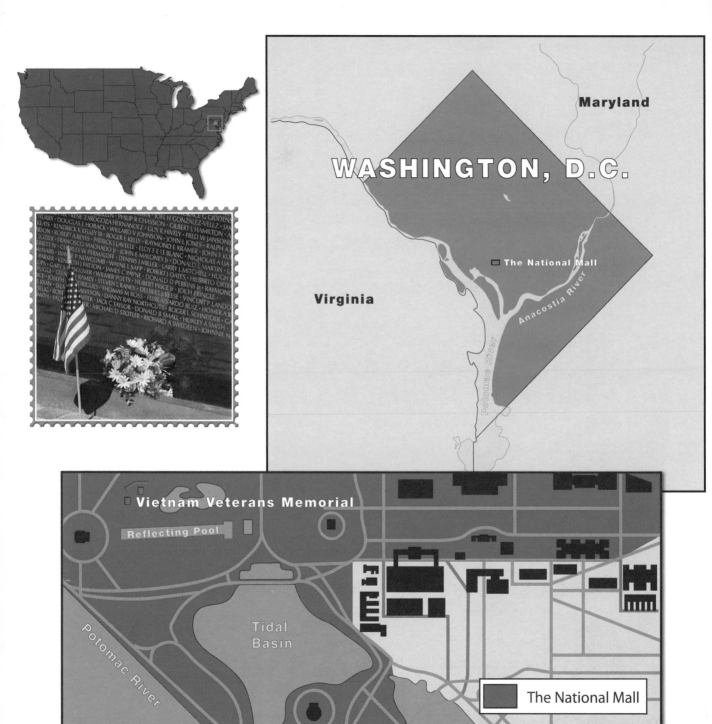

Maryland

WASHINGTON, D.C.

Virginia

☐ The National Mall

Anacostia River

Potomac River

☐ Vietnam Veterans Memorial

Reflecting Pool

Tidal Basin

Potomac River

The National Mall

The Vietnam Veterans Memorial is in Washington, D.C. This city is the capital of the United States.

The Vietnam Veterans Memorial has three sections. The first section is The Wall. It has two walls shaped like triangles that meet to form a "V." The names of U.S. soldiers who died during the Vietnam War (1957–1975) are carved into the granite walls. More than 58,000 names are listed. The Wall was built in 1982.

The Three Servicemen statue is the memorial's second part. It was added in 1984. The statue shows three soldiers walking out of the jungle. They face The Wall. A flagpole is near the statue. It has five seals, or symbols, on the base. The seals stand for the Army, Air Force, Marine Corps, Navy, and Coast Guard.

The Vietnam Women's Memorial is the third part. This statue was added in 1993. It shows nurses helping wounded soldiers. Nearby, eight trees remind visitors of the eight nurses who died in Vietnam. The nurses' names also are on The Wall.

The Vietnam Veterans Memorial is in Washington, D.C.

The Idea for the Memorial

Jan saw the monuments in Washington, D.C. Some monuments honored important leaders such as Abraham Lincoln and George Washington. Jan wanted to honor all the soldiers who served in Vietnam.

In May 1979, Jan started a special committee. He and others began the Vietnam Veterans Memorial Fund (VVMF). This committee began to raise money for the memorial. Jan put in $2,800 of his own money.

Jan and the committee asked people to give money. He reminded people that more than 58,000 Americans died in the Vietnam War. Many more were injured. Nearly three million Americans served in the war. A memorial would help Americans remember all those who served in the war.

Jan's committee raised $8 million. Next, they needed a place to build the monument. Senators sent a bill to Congress. The bill asked for land on the National Mall between the Washington Monument and the Lincoln Memorial. Congress passed the bill.

Jan Scruggs (left) received support for building the Vietnam Veterans Memorial from Senators John Warner (middle) and Charles "Mac" Mathias Jr. (right).

Designing the Memorial

The VVMF needed a design for the monument. The committee had four rules. The memorial should make people think about the war. It should fit with the surrounding area. The monument must list the names of all those who died during the Vietnam War. It should not try to prove whether the war was right or wrong.

The committee held a contest. People from all over the United States sent in their designs. The committee studied more than 1,400 drawings. They chose a sketch by 21-year-old Maya Ying Lin. Maya was from Ohio. She was a student at Yale University.

Maya's design showed a wall shaped like a "V." The names of each person who died in Vietnam would be carved into the wall. Her drawing showed one end of the wall facing the Lincoln Memorial. The other end pointed toward the Washington Monument.

Maya Ying Lin (left) designed The Wall.

ES W ADAMS · ROY O BUCHANAN
ROBERT L DANCE · PEDRO DE HER
GUS · DENNIS J GREEN · LOUIE E H
O McDONALD · RICHARD J NOLE
A · GEORGE W PIERCE · HENRY L PIF
EL R SMART · JESSIE JAMES TYLER · H
PAUL A DE VEGTER · PHILIP G DES L
GOURLEY · RONALD J JANOUSEK
RD E BECK Jr · DONALD H McMAIN
AN STRIBBLING · STEPHEN A YOUN
G · RONALD L BERRY · DAVID E CAR
NALD L ELLIOTT · STEPHEN GLOWE
HILLIARD · ROGER D HOLLIFIELD
T MARMIE · WILLIAM E MICKELSEN
EK · CARL A PETERSON · PAUL G PI

Building the Memorial

On March 26, 1982, the VVMF held a groundbreaking ceremony. This ceremony celebrated the beginning of work on the memorial. The VVMF had 120 shovels for their special guests. Veterans from all 50 states dug into the ground.

Workers in India dug large blocks of black granite for the memorial. The stone was shipped to Barre, Vermont. Workers there polished the stone. It shone like a mirror. They cut the stone into panels.

Next, the panels went to Memphis, Tennessee. Glass workers carved 57,939 names of the men and women who died in Vietnam. Most of them had died in battle. Some soldiers still were missing. Workers carved a plus sign next to the names of the missing. They carved a diamond next to the names of the dead.

Some veterans wanted a statue instead of The Wall. The VVMF decided to build both. In July 1982, the VVMF hired Frederick Hart to make a statue. Hart's statue would be part of the Memorial.

A diamond appears next to the names of those people who died in Vietnam.

Opening Ceremonies

Americans held a ceremony to open the Vietnam Veterans Memorial on November 13, 1982. Veterans from every state paraded along Constitution Avenue. High school bands played. A group called Gold Star Mothers also marched. Members of this group lost their sons or daughters in the war.

Speakers and special guests sat on a platform. Maya Ying Lin was one of the guests. Jan Scruggs spoke. "I know our country appreciates our service," he said.

More than 150,000 people gathered at the memorial. The crowd rushed to The Wall. They looked for names of friends. They touched the names of family members. They hugged and cried. They would always remember those who died in the war. The memorial also would help other Americans remember them.

Opening ceremonies for the Vietnam Veterans Memorial were held on November 13, 1982.

The Memorial Changes

The statue was finished in 1984. It was called *The Three Servicemen*. The men in the statue look like they are walking from the jungle. They face The Wall. One soldier is black. One is white. One is Hispanic. The statue shows that many races fought in the war.

Officials put up a flagpole near the statue. The flagpole is 60 feet (18 meters) tall. An American flag flies from the pole 24 hours a day.

In 1984, a group of women started the Vietnam Women's Memorial Project. They wanted a memorial for the women who went to Vietnam. Nearly 10,000 women worked as nurses and in other jobs in Vietnam. Eight women died during the war. Their names appear on The Wall.

The Vietnam Women's Memorial shows three nurses. One is looking at the sky. Another nurse is helping a soldier. A third nurse holds a helmet. The Vietnam Women's Memorial was dedicated on November 11, 1993. It completes the Vietnam Veterans Memorial.

Three nurses and a soldier make up the Vietnam Women's Memorial. The third nurse faces the other direction.

Visiting the Memorial

The Vietnam Veterans Memorial is open 24 hours a day. From 8:00 a.m. to midnight, National Park Service rangers help people locate names. People sometimes make rubbings of names. They use paper and a pencil to trace over names on The Wall.

Many visitors leave keepsakes near the memorial. People leave notes, medals, flowers, or flags. The Park Service collects and stores these items. Museums sometimes display the keepsakes. People have left more than 60,000 items at The Wall since 1982.

The VVMF wanted to show The Wall to people who cannot travel to Washington, D.C. In 1996, the group built a model of The Wall. It is half the size of the real Wall. It travels all over the United States. Veterans groups often sponsor visits of "The Traveling Wall." They call it *The Wall That Heals*.

The Vietnam Veterans Memorial helps people remember the soldiers who fought in the Vietnam War. It is the most visited memorial in Washington, D.C.

Visitors at The Wall often make rubbings of names.

Important Dates

★ 1957–1975—The Vietnam War

★ 1979—Jan Scruggs organizes the Vietnam Veterans Memorial Fund (VVMF).

★ 1980—The U.S. Congress gives permission for a site near the Lincoln Memorial.

★ 1981—The VVMF holds a memorial design competition.

★ 1982—The VVMF approves Maya Ying Lin's design.
Builders start The Wall on March 26.
Workers finish The Wall in October.
The Vietnam Veterans Memorial is dedicated on November 13.

★ 1984—The Vietnam Women's Memorial Project is started by a group of women.
Workers add *The Three Servicemen* statue and a flagpole to the Vietnam Veterans Memorial.

★ 1992—The National Park Service and the Smithsonian Institution display items that people have left at the Memorial.

★ 1993—The Vietnam Women's Memorial statue arrives on November 1.
The Vietnam Women's Memorial is dedicated on November 11.

★ 1996—The VVMF builds a model, "The Traveling Wall."

★ 1997—People honor the 15th anniversary of The Wall.

Words to Know

ceremony (SER-uh-moh-nee)—formal actions, words, or music that honor a person or an event

committee (kuh-MIT-ee)—a group of people chosen to do a special task

keepsake (KEEP-sayk)—something kept for a memory

monument (MON-yuh-muhnt)—a statue or building that is meant to remind people of an event or a person

sculpture (SKUHLP-chur)—something carved or shaped out of stone, metal, marble, clay, or another material

veteran (VET-ur-uhn)—someone who has served in the armed forces; many veterans served during the Vietnam War.

Read More

Ashabranner, Brent. *Their Names to Live: What the Vietnam Veterans Memorial Means to America.* Brookfield, Conn.: Twenty-First Century Books, 1998.

Cooper, Jason. *Vietnam Veterans Memorial.* American Landmarks. Vero Beach, Fla.: Rourke, 1999.

Useful Addresses

The Vietnam Veterans Memorial Fund
1023 15th Street NW
Second Floor
Washington, DC 20005

Vietnam Women's Memorial Project
2001 S Street NW
Suite 610
Washington, DC 20009

Internet Sites

Vietnam Veterans Memorial Fund
http://www.vvmf.org
Vietnam Veterans Memorial
http://www.nps.gov/vive/home.htm
Vietnam Women's Memorial Project
http://www.vietnamwomensmemorial.org/pages/index2.html
The Virtual Wall
http://www.thevirtualwall.org
The Wall Questions and Answers
http://www.telepath.com/seanair/wallfaq.html

Index

4 - 1/07